The Ultimate
5 Ingredient
Cookbook

Hannie P. Scott

www.Hanniepscott.com

99

One of the very nicest things about life is the way we must regularly stop whatever we are doing and devote our attention to eating.

LUCIANO PAVAROTTI

CONTENTS

BREAKFAST RECIPES

SIDES

MAIN DISHES

DESSERTS

FREE GIFT

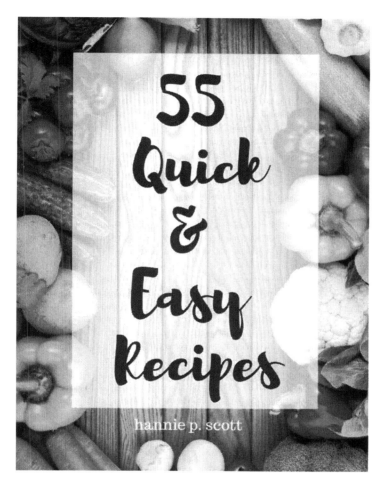

Breakfast, Lunch, Dinner, Soups, Salads, Desserts and More!

To download your free eBook, simply visit:
www.Hanniepscott.com/freegift

BREAKFAST RECIPES

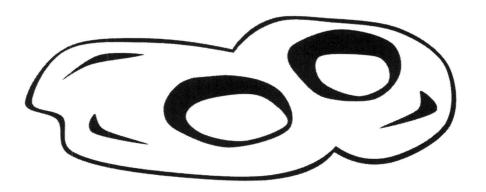

Brown Sugar Bacon

Serves: 4-6

What you need:

- 1 package bacon

- 1 cup brown sugar

- 1 tsp cayenne pepper

What to do:

1. Preheat your oven to 375 degrees F.
2. Line a large baking sheet with foil.
3. In a shallow bowl, mix together the brown sugar and cayenne pepper.
4. Dredge the bacon in the brown sugar mixture and lay each slice on the foil lined pan.
5. Bake for 15-20 minutes or until bacon is crisp.
6. Cool on a wire rack.

Egg in a Nest

Serves: 4

What you need:

- 2 slices of bread

- 2 tbsp butter

- 2 eggs

- Salt and pepper, to taste

What to do:

1. Add the butter to a medium sized skillet over medium heat.
2. Cut a hole from the center of each slice of bread. You can use a drinking glass or a cookie cutter.
3. Place the bread slices in the pan and toast for a minute or two then flip.
4. Crack an egg into the center of each piece of toast.
5. Cook until the eggs are set.
6. Sprinkle with salt and pepper before serving.

Cinnamon Roll Waffles

Serves: 4

What you need:

- 1 can cinnamon roll dough

What to do:

1. Heat your waffle maker.
2. Separate the cinnamon rolls and set aside the icing.
3. Spray your heated waffle maker and place one roll in and close the lid. Cook for about 2-3 minutes or until cinnamon roll is cooked through. Repeat until all cinnamon rolls are done.
4. Remove the lid from the icing and microwave the icing for 15-20 seconds.
5. Drizzle the icing over the cinnamon roll waffles before serving.

Easy Powdered Sugar Donuts

Serves: 6-8

What you need:

- 2 7.5-oz rolls of canned biscuits

- 2 cups powdered sugar

- Canola oil

What to do:

1. Pour an inch of canola oil into a heavy skillet and heat over medium heat on your stove.
2. Place a sheet of wax paper or parchment paper on your counter.
3. Unroll the biscuits and place them on the paper.
4. With a rolling pin or a jar, flatten out each biscuit.
5. Use a plastic bottle cap and make a donut hole in the center of each flattened roll.
6. When the oil is hot, place a few donuts in the skillet at a time. Don't overcrowd the skillet.
7. Let them cook for a minute or two and flip them with a fork.
8. Cook on each side until the donuts are golden brown, then transfer to a plate lined with paper towels to drain off some of the oil.

9. Place two cups of powdered sugar in a gallon zip lock bag.

10. After all of the donuts are cooked, place a few of them at a time in the zip lock bag, seal the bag and shake until they are covered completely.

11. Remove the donuts from the bag and repeat until all donuts are covered.

12. Serve warm.

Sausage Breakfast Casserole

Serves: 4-6

What you need:

- 1 package of crescent rolls

- 1 lb ground sausage, browned and drained

- 6 eggs, beaten

- 2 cups shredded cheddar cheese

What to do:

1. Preheat your oven to 350 degrees F.
2. Spray a 9x13 inch pan with non-stick cooking spray.
3. Roll the crescent rolls into the bottom of the pan.
4. Top the rolls with the sausage in an even layer.
5. Evenly pour the eggs over the sausage.
6. Sprinkle the cheese evenly over the sausage and eggs.
7. Bake for 30 minutes or until eggs are set.

Sausage, Egg, and Cheese Roll-Ups

Serves: 6-8

What you need:

- 5 eggs

- 1 can crescent rolls

- 8 fully cooked sausage links

- 4 slices cheese

- Salt and pepper, to taste

What to do:

1. Heat your oven to 350 degrees F.
2. Line a baking pan with parchment paper.
3. Beat the eggs in a small bowl and scramble all but 2 tbsp of them.
4. Unroll the crescent rolls onto the parchment paper.
5. Cut the cheese slices in half and place a half on each roll.
6. Top each slice of cheese with a spoonful of scrambled eggs and 1 sausage link.
7. Loosely roll up the crescent rolls.
8. Brush each roll with the reserved eggs and sprinkle with salt and pepper.
9. Bake for 15-18 minutes or until the rolls are golden-brown.

Scrambled Eggs

Serves: 1-2

What you need:

- 1 tbsp butter
- 3 eggs
- 1/4 tsp salt
- 1/2 tsp butter
- 1/4 tsp black pepper

What to do:

1. Melt 1 tbsp of butter in a 10-inch non-stick skillet over medium-low heat.
2. Crack 3 eggs into a medium bowl and gently whisk with a fork until the whites and yolks are barely combined.
3. Pour the eggs into the skillet.
4. Let the eggs sit in the skillet until they begin to stick to the bottom of the skillet, about 30 seconds.
5. Begin stirring the eggs with a wooden spoon. Stir for 3-4 minutes.
6. Add 1/4 tsp of salt, 1/2 tsp of butter, 1/4 tsp of black pepper to the eggs and stir and cook for another 1-2 minutes.

7. Transfer to a plate and serve.

Slow Cooker Cinnamon Roll Casserole

Servings: 6-8

What you need:

- 2 12-oz tubes of cinnamon rolls, cut into 4 pieces each
- 4 eggs
- 1/2 cup whipping cream
- 3 tbsp maple syrup
- 2 tsp vanilla

What to do:

1. Spray your slow cooker with cooking spray or line it with a liner.
2. Place half of the cinnamon roll pieces into the bottom of your slow cooker. Make sure the bottom is completely covered.
3. In a small bowl, whisk together the eggs, cream, syrup, and vanilla.
4. Pour the mixture over the cinnamon rolls.
5. Place the remaining cinnamon roll pieces in the slow cooker and spoon 1 packet of the icing over the top.

6. Cook on low for 3 hours or until the sides are golden brown.
7. Drizzle the other packet of icing over the top before serving.

Slow Cooker French Toast

Servings: 4-6

What you need:

- 1/2 loaf of cinnamon bread
- 6 eggs
- 1 cup milk
- 1 tbsp brown sugar
- 1 tsp vanilla

What to do:

1. Spray your slow cooker with non-stick cooking spray.
2. In a large mixing bowl, whisk together the eggs, milk, brown sugar, and vanilla.
3. Dip each slice of bread into the egg mixture and then place it in your slow cooker.
4. Pour any remaining egg mixture on top of the bread in the slow cooker.
5. Cook on low 6-8 hours.
6. Serve with fresh fruit, whipped cream, or syrup.

Slow Cooker Pancake Bake

Servings: 4-6

What you need:

- 1 cup Bisquick

- 1/2 cup milk

- 1 egg

- 1/3 cup sugar

- 1 tbsp cinnamon

What to do:

1. Spray your slow cooker with nonstick spray or a place a liner in it.
2. In a medium bowl, whisk together the Bisquick, milk, and egg until there are no lumps.
3. Stir together the cinnamon and sugar in another bowl.
4. Pour the Bisquick mixture into the bottom of your slow cooker.
5. Sprinkle the cinnamon and sugar mixture over the top.
6. Cook for 1 hour to 1 1/2 hours or until the center is cooked through.

Southwestern Scrambled Eggs

Serves: 1-2

What you need:

- 3 eggs

- 1 tbsp milk

- 1/4 cup shredded cheese

- 1/4 cup black beans

- 1/4 cup salsa

What to do:

1. Spray a non-stick skillet with cooking spray and heat over medium-high heat.
2. Crack the eggs into a small bowl and whisk with a fork. Stir in the milk.
3. Pour the eggs into the heated pan.
4. When the eggs begin to cook, begin to stir them with a wooden spoon.
5. Add the black beans and continue to stir.
6. When eggs are done, transfer them to a plate.
7. Top with salsa and serve.

Waffle Biscuits

Serves: 4

What you need:

- 1 8-count can of flaky biscuits

- 4 eggs, fried or scrambled

- 4 slices of cheese

- 8 slices of bacon, cooked

What to do:

1. Heat and spray your waffle maker with non-stick spray.
2. Unroll the biscuits from the can.
3. Place one biscuit in the center of your waffle maker, close the lid and cook for 2-3 minutes or until the biscuit is golden-brown. Repeat until all 8 biscuits are cooked.
4. Place 1 egg, 1 slice of cheese, and 2 slices of bacon on a waffle biscuit and top with another waffle biscuit. Repeat until you have assembled 4 waffle biscuits.
5. Serve warm.

SIDES

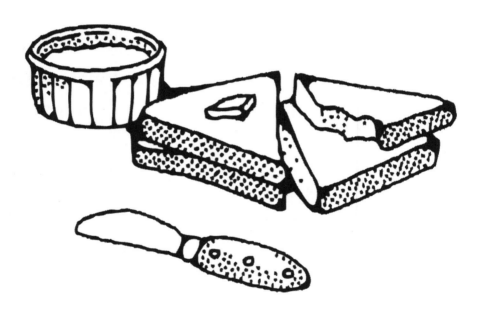

Strawberry Bacon Salad

Serves: 2-4

What you need:

- 1/2 head of romaine lettuce

- 4 cups spinach

- 1/2 cup toasted almonds

- 8-10 slices of cooked bacon, crumbled

- 2 cups sliced strawberries

What to do:

1. Chop the romaine lettuce into small pieces and place in a large bowl.
2. Mix the almonds and bacon crumbles into the bowl with the lettuce.
3. Add strawberries just before serving.
4. Serve with poppy seed dressing.

Buffalo Chicken Dip

Servings: 8-10

What you need:

- 3 chicken breasts, cooked and shredded

- 8 oz cream cheese, softened

- 1 cup ranch dressing

- 1 cup Frank's hot sauce

- 1 cup shredded cheddar cheese

What to do:

1. Mix together the cream cheese, ranch dressing, hot sauce, and cheddar cheese in a slow cooker.
2. Place shredded chicken into the mixture and combine.
3. Place the lid on the slow cooker and heat on high for 30 minutes-1 hour.
4. Pour it into a serving dish when ready to serve.
5. This can be served with veggie slices, chips, crackers, etc.

Slow Cooker Spinach Queso Dip

Serves: 6-8

What you need:

- 10 oz frozen chopped spinach, thawed and drained well

- 1 lb Velveeta cheese

- 8 oz cream cheese

- 1 jar salsa

What to do:

1. Cut the Velveeta and cream cheese into cubes and place them into a slow cooker.
2. Add in the spinach and salsa.
3. Cook for 3-4 hours on low, stirring every hour or so.
4. Serve with tortilla chips.

Cheesy Broccoli

Servings: 6-8

What you need:

- 2 12-oz packages of frozen broccoli florets

- 2 cans cheddar cheese soup

- 1 cup shredded cheddar cheese

- 1/2 tsp salt

- 1/2 tsp pepper

What to do:

1. Place all of the ingredients into your slow cooker.
2. Cook on low for 6 hours or on high for 3 hours. Stir occasionally.

Cheesy Buffalo Cauliflower

Servings: 6-8

What you need:

- 2 12-oz packages of frozen cauliflower florets

- 2 cans cheddar cheese soup

- 1 cup shredded cheddar cheese

- 1/2 cup Frank's Red Hot Buffalo Wing Sauce

- 1/2 tsp pepper

What to do:

1. Place all of the ingredients into your slow cooker.
2. Cook on low for 6 hours or on high for 3 hours. Stir occasionally.

Cheesy Cauliflower

Servings: 6-8

What you need:

- 2 12-oz packages of frozen cauliflower florets

- 2 cans cheddar cheese soup

- 1 cup shredded cheddar cheese

- 1/2 tsp salt

- 1/2 tsp pepper

What to do:

1. Place all of the ingredients into your slow cooker.
2. Cook on low for 6 hours or on high for 3 hours. Stir occasionally.

Mashed Cauliflower

Servings: 2-4

What you need:

- 1 head of cauliflower

- 1 clove garlic, minced

- 2 tbsp butter

- Salt and pepper, to taste

What to do:

1. Cut the cauliflower into medium sized florets.
2. Place the florets into a soup pot and cover them with water.
3. Bring the water to a boil and keep it at a medium boil for 15-20 minutes.
4. Drain the water from the pot and turn the heat to low.
5. Mast the cauliflower in the pot with a potato masher.
6. Add the garlic, butter, salt, and pepper and stir well.

Kale Chips

Servings: 4

What you need:

- 1 bunch kale, washed and thoroughly dried

- 1 tbsp olive oil

- 2 tsp sea salt

- ½ lemon

What to do:

1. Preheat your oven to 300 degrees F.
2. Strip the kale from the stems and break into it pieces.
3. In a large bowl, combine the kale with olive oil and salt.
4. Spread kale evenly on large baking sheet.
5. Bake for 20 minutes or until kale is crispy.
6. Remove from oven and squeeze lemon juice over the kale chips (watch for seeds!)
7. Serve immediately.

Roasted Cauliflower

Servings: 4-6

What you need:

- 1 large head of cauliflower

- 3 tbsp olive oil

- 1 clove garlic, minced

- 1 tsp sea salt

- 2 tbsp grated parmesan cheese

What to do:

1. Preheat your oven to 350 degrees F.
2. Spray a baking dish with non-stick cooking spray.
3. Trim the stem of the cauliflower so that it is even with the cauliflower florets and the cauliflower sits flat.
4. In a small bowl, stir together the olive oil and the garlic.
5. Brush the bottom of the cauliflower with the olive oil/garlic mixture then season with salt.
6. Lay the cauliflower flat in the baking dish and brush the top and sides with the olive oil mixture and season with salt and parmesan cheese.

7. Bake for 55 minutes to 1 hour or until the center of the cauliflower is tender when pierced with a knife.
8. Slice into wedges before serving.

Slow Cooker Broccoli Casserole

Serves: 6-8

What you need:

- 2 12-oz bags of frozen broccoli florets

- 2 cans cheddar cheese soup

- 1 cup shredded cheddar cheese

- Salt and pepper, to taste

What to do:

1. Slightly thaw the broccoli.
2. Combine all of the ingredients in a large bowl.
3. Pour mixture into a slow cooker and cook on high for 2-3 hours or until hot and bubbly.

Veggie Wrap

Servings: 1

What you need:

- 1 low carb wrap

- 3 tbsp cream cheese

- 2 cups chopped veggies

- 1 tbsp lemon juice

What to do:

1. Spread cream cheese on the wrap.
2. Chop all the veggies into small pieces and place them in a large bowl.
3. Spritz veggies with lemon juice to preserve colors (and for flavor!).
4. Place the veggies on wrap and roll it up.
5. Cut the wrap in half or in thirds.

Zucchini Chips

Servings: 2-4

What you need:

- 1 large zucchini

- 1 tsp olive oil

- Salt to taste

What to do:

1. Very thinly slice the zucchini.
2. Place slices on baking sheet.
3. Brush on the olive oil.
4. Bake at 225 degrees F for 2 hours.

Macaroni and Cheese

Servings: 8-10

What you need:

- 16 oz elbow macaroni

- 3 cups milk

- 8-oz Velveeta cheese, cubed

- 1/2 stick of butter, sliced

- 4 cups shredded cheddar cheese

What to do:

1. Cook the pasta in boiling water for 3 minutes ONLY. Drain and rinse well.
2. Place the pasta into your crock pot and add in the rest of the ingredients.
3. Cook on low for 2-3 hours, stirring occasionally.

Slow Cooker Bacon Ranch Potatoes

Servings: 8

What you need:

- 6 slices of bacon

- 3 lbs red potatoes, chopped

- 1 1/2 cups shredded cheddar cheese

- 1 tbsp ranch seasoning

- 2 tbsp chopped chives

What to do:

1. Cook and crumble the bacon.
2. Place the potatoes into the slow cooker and sprinkle them with cheese, ranch seasoning, and bacon.
3. Cover and cook for 7-8 hours on low or 4 hours on high.
4. Serve garnished with chives.

Slow Cooker Sweet Potatoes

Serves: 4

What you need:

- 4 medium sized sweet potatoes

- Butter

- Brown sugar

- Mini marshmallows

What to do:

1. Scrub, wash, and dry the sweet potatoes.
2. Poke each potato with a fork several times.
3. Wrap each potato in foil twice.
4. Place potatoes in slow cooker and cook on high for 4 hours or on low for 8 hours.
5. Top with butter, brown sugar, and mini marshmallows before serving.

Slow Cooker Corn on the Cob

Serves: 6

What you need:

- 6 ears of corn

- 1/2 stick of butter

- Salt and pepper, to taste

What to do:

1. Lightly spread butter on each corn cob.
2. Sprinkle each cob with salt and pepper.
3. Wrap each corn cob in aluminum foil.
4. Place them all in the slow cooker and cook for 2 hours.

Slow Cooker Cheddar Creamed Corn

Serves: 6-8

What you need:

- 32-oz of frozen corn
- 1 8-oz block of cream cheese, cubed
- 1 cup shredded cheddar cheese
- 1/4 cup butter
- 1/2 cup heavy cream

What to do:

1. Place all of the ingredients in your slow cooker and stir well.
2. Cook on low for 3-4 hours or until cream cheese is melted.
3. Stir well and serve.

Broccoli Cheese Soup

Servings: 4-6

What you need:

- 4 cups chicken broth

- 2 cups chopped broccoli florets

- 1 small onion, diced

- 15 oz evaporated milk

- 2 cups shredded cheddar cheese

What to do:

1. Place all of the ingredients except the cheese in your slow cooker. Cook on low for 6 hours.
2. Add in the cheese and cook for an additional 30 minutes or until the cheese is melted.

MAIN DISHES

Barbeque Chicken Legs

Servings: 4-6

What you need:

- 3 lbs chicken legs

- 2 cups of your favorite barbeque sauce

- Garlic powder

- Cajun Seasoning

- Salt and pepper

What to do:

1. Preheat your oven to 350 degrees F.
2. Pat the chicken dry with a paper towel and season well with garlic powder, Cajun seasoning, salt and pepper.
3. Place the chicken on a rack inside of a roasting pan.
4. Cover the roasting pan and bake for 45 minutes.
5. Remove the chicken from the oven and brush each piece generously with barbeque sauce.
6. Bake uncovered for 30 more minutes.
7. Increase the heat to 450 degrees and cook for another 5 minutes.

Beef Fajitas

Servings: 6

What you need:

- 1 onion, diced
- 3 bell peppers, sliced (I used various colors)
- 2 lbs thin sliced beef, cut into strips
- 1 package fajita seasoning

What to do:

1. Place the onions, peppers, and beef into your slow cooker.
2. Sprinkle the fajita seasoning over the mixture.
3. Cook on high for 5 hours or on low for 8 hours.

Buffalo Chicken Sliders

Servings: 10

What you need:

- 3 chicken breasts

- 1 12-oz bottle of buffalo wing sauce, divided

- 1 package of ranch seasoning mix

- 2 packs of Hawaiian rolls

- 1 package coleslaw mix

What to do:

1. Place the chicken breasts into your slow cooker and pour in ¾ of the wing sauce and all of the ranch seasoning mix. Cover and cook for 6-7 hours or until the chicken easily shreds.
2. Once the chicken is cooked, drain off the liquid.
3. Add rest of the buffalo sauce and shred the chicken with two forks.
4. Spoon the shredded chicken onto Hawaiian rolls, top with coleslaw mix, and serve.

Chicken and Cheese Rolls

Servings: 6

What you need:

- 1 package 6-count refrigerated crescent rolls

- 2 cups chopped cooked chicken

- 2 cups shredded cheddar cheese

- 1 10.75-oz can of cream of chicken soup

- 1 cup of milk

What to do:

1. Preheat your oven to 350 degrees F and spray a baking dish with non-stick spray.
2. Separate the crescent rolls and unroll them onto a clean surface.
3. In a medium bowl, mix together the cream of chicken soup and milk.
4. Place a spoonful of chicken and a spoonful of cheese on the large part of each crescent roll.
5. Roll each crescent roll up and pinch the seal together.
6. Place each roll in the prepared baking dish.
7. Pour the soup mixture over the rolls.
8. Bake for 30 minutes.

Chicken and Gravy

Servings: 6

What you need:

- 6 boneless, skinless chicken breasts

- 1 onion, diced

- 2 cans cream of chicken soup

- 3 tbsp soy sauce

- Cooked rice

What to do:

1. Place all of the ingredients except the rice into your slow cooker.
2. Cook on low for 8 hours or on high for 5 hours.
3. Stir and serve over rice.

Chicken and Waffle Sliders

Servings: 6

What you need:

- 12 frozen mini waffles, toasted

- 6 chicken tenders, cooked

- Maple syrup

- Toothpicks

What to do:

1. Slice the cooked chicken tenders into thirds.
2. Sandwich 1 piece of chicken between two mini waffles and secure with a toothpick.
3. Serve with maple syrup.

Chicken Cordon Bleu

Servings: 6

What you need:

- 6 thin sliced chicken breasts

- 1/3 lb thinly sliced black forest ham

- 1/3 lb thinly sliced Swiss cheese

- Salt and pepper, to taste

What to do:

1. Preheat your oven to 350 degrees F.
2. Lay the chicken breasts out on a large cutting board or other clean working surface.
3. Season each breast with salt and pepper.
4. Lay 1-2 slices of ham on each breast.
5. Lay 2 slices of cheese on top of the ham.
6. Roll up each chicken breast tightly and secure with toothpicks.
7. Place each rolled up chicken breast onto a baking pan and bake for 30-35 minutes.

Honey Chicken

Servings: 4-6

What you need:

- 4 chicken breasts

- 1/3 cup melted butter

- 1/3 cup honey

- 2 tbsp spicy brown mustard

- 1/4 tsp salt

What to do:

1. Preheat your oven to 350 degrees F.
2. Place the chicken breasts in a shallow square baking pan.
3. Combine the butter, honey, mustard, and salt in a small bowl. Pour this mixture over the chicken.
4. Bake for 1 hour or to a minimal internal temperature of 165 degrees F. Baste every 15 minutes while baking.

Garlic Alfredo Chicken

Servings: 4

What you need:

- 4 boneless, skinless chicken breasts

- 3 cloves garlic, minced

- 2 15-oz jars alfredo sauce

- 1 package bowtie pasta

What to do:

1. Add the chicken and minced garlic to your slow cooker and cook on high for 3 hours.
2. Drain the juices from the slow cooker.
3. Pour the alfredo sauce onto the chicken in the slow cooker. Cook on high for 30 minutes.
4. Cook and drain pasta according to package directions.
5. Serve chicken and sauce over pasta.

Honey Mustard Chicken

Servings: 4

What you need:

- 4 boneless, skinless chicken breasts
- 1 12-oz bottle of Dijon mustard
- 1/2 cup honey

What to do:

1. Cook the chicken in your slow cooker on high for 3 hours or on low for 6 hours.
2. Drain the juices from the crock pot.
3. In a small bowl, mix together the honey and the Dijon mustard.
4. Pour the mixture over the chicken, gently stir, then cook for another hour.

Maple Mustard Baked Chicken

Servings: 4-6

What you need:

- 4 chicken breasts

- 1/2 cup spicy brown mustard

- 1/4 cup maple syrup

- 1 tbsp red wine vinegar

- Salt and pepper, to taste

What to do:

1. Preheat your oven to 425 degrees F.
2. In a medium sized bowl, mix together the mustard, syrup, and vinegar.
3. Place the chicken into a 9x13 baking dish and season with salt and pepper.
4. Pour the mustard mixture over the chicken.
5. Bake for 30-40 minutes or until the internal temperature of the chicken reaches 165 degrees F.

Honey Mustard Pork Chops

Servings: 6

What you need:

- 1 1/2 lbs boneless pork chops

- 1 onion, sliced

- 3 tbsp honey

- 3 tbsp Dijon mustard

- 1/2 tsp black pepper

What to do:

1. Place the pork chops and onions in your slow cooker.
2. In a small bowl, stir together the honey, mustard, and pepper.
3. Pour the honey mustard mixture over the pork chops.
4. Cook on low for 4 hours or on high for 8 hours.

Chicken Curry

Servings: 8

What you need:

- 3 lbs chicken thighs

- 1 onion, chopped

- 3 tbsp curry

- 1 can unsweetened coconut milk

- 16-oz jar of salsa

What to do:

1. Place all of the ingredients except the coconut milk into your crock pot.
2. Cook on low for 8 hours or on high for 4 hours.
3. Remove the chicken to a serving plate.
4. Whisk the coconut milk into the liquid left in the slow cooker.
5. Serve the chicken with the sauce over the top.

Chicken Fingers

Servings: 4

What you need:

- 4 chicken breasts, cut into strips

- 1 egg, beaten

- 1 cup all-purpose flour

- 2 tsp Cajun seasoning

What to do:

1. Preheat your oven to 425 degrees F and line a baking sheet with parchment paper.
2. In a shallow dish, combine the flour with the Cajun seasoning.
3. Place the beaten egg in a separate shallow dish.
4. Dip each chicken strip into the egg then the flour mixture until well coated.
5. Place strips on the baking sheet and bake for 18-20 minutes. Turn once halfway through cooking.

Chicken Salad

Servings: 2

What you need:

- 1 cup cooked and shredded chicken breast

- 2 tbsp pickle relish

- 1/3 cup mayonnaise

- 1/4 tsp paprika

- Salt and pepper, to taste

What to do:

1. In a large bowl, combine all ingredients.
2. Mix very well, until everything is combined.
3. Cover and refrigerate for at least 2 hours.

Easy Italian Baked Chicken

Servings: 4-6

What you need:

- 4 chicken breasts

- 1 packet dry Italian dressing mix

- 1/2 cup packed brown sugar

What to do:

1. Preheat your oven to 350 degrees and line a 9x13 baking dish with aluminum foil.
2. In a small bowl, mix together the Italian dressing mix and the brown sugar.
3. Place the chicken breasts between two sheets of wax or parchment paper and pound them until they are thin.
4. Cut each chicken breast in half.
5. Dip each piece of chicken into the Italian dressing/sugar mixture and coat well.
6. Place the chicken into the baking pan.
7. Sprinkle any remaining seasoning mixture onto the chicken.
8. Bake for 20-30 minutes or until the internal temp is 165 degrees F. Flip the chicken over after about 15 minutes.

9. Broil the chicken on each side for 1-2 minutes before removing from the oven.

Meatball Sliders

Makes 24 sliders

What you need:

- 24-count fully cooked frozen meatballs

- 1 18-oz jar grape jelly

- 1 12-oz jar chili sauce

- 24 rolls or slider buns

- Cheese slices

What to do:

1. In your slow cooker, stir together the grape jelly and chili sauce.
2. Add the frozen meatballs to the mixture in your slow cooker and stir.
3. Cook on high for 3 hours or on low for 6 hours.
4. Serve on slider buns topped with cheese.

Mexican Chicken

Servings: 1-2

What you need:

- 4 chicken breasts

- 1 tbsp taco seasoning

- 1/2 cup enchilada sauce

- 1 cup shredded cheddar cheese

- 3 green onions, chopped

What to do:

1. Add the chicken, taco seasoning, and enchilada sauce to a slow cooker and cook on low for 4-6 hours.
2. Shred chicken with a fork.
3. Stir in cheese and cook for another hour.
4. Stir in green onions before serving.

Mexican Chicken II

Servings: 4

What you need:

- 4 boneless, skinless chicken breasts

- 1 16-oz jar of salsa

- 1 15-oz can black beans, drained and rinsed

- 1 package taco seasoning

What to do:

1. Place all of the ingredients except the black beans into your slow cooker.
2. Cook on low for 8 hours. Stir every 2 hours.
3. One hour before serving, pour in the black beans.

Shredded Buffalo Chicken

Servings: 2-4

What you need:

- 4 chicken breasts

- 12 oz bottle of buffalo wing sauce

- 2 tbsp ranch mix

- 2 tbsp butter

- 2 cloves garlic, minced

What to do:

1. Place the chicken breasts in a slow cooker.
2. Pour the wing sauce over the chicken.
3. Sprinkle ranch mix over the sauce.
4. Add butter and garlic to the slow cooker.
5. Cook on low for 4-6 hours or until chicken shreds easily.
6. Remove chicken from the slow cooker and shred it completely.
7. Put the shredded chicken back into the slow cooker and cook on low for another hour before serving.

Slow Cooker 5-ingredient Chili

Servings: 6

What you need:

- 1 lb ground beef, browned and drained

- 3 15-oz cans rotel tomatoes

- 2 15-oz cans beans, drained (kidney or chili or both)

- 1 small white onion, diced

- 2 tbsp chili powder

What to do:

1. Add all of the ingredients to your slow cooker.
2. Cook on low for 6 hours.

Slow Cooker Apricot Orange Chicken

Servings: 4

What you need:

- 4 boneless, skinless chicken breasts

- 1 18-oz jar apricot preserves

- 1 cup orange juice

- 1 package onion soup mix

What to do:

1. Place the chicken in your slow cooker.
2. Stir together the preserves, orange juice, and onion soup mix in a small bowl.
3. Pour the mixture over the chicken.
4. Cook on low for 6 hours or until the chicken is very tender.

Slow Cooker BBQ Ribs

Servings: 4

What you need:

- 2 1/2 lb rack of baby back pork ribs

- 1 tbsp brown sugar

- Salt and pepper

- 1 1/2 cups BBQ sauce

What to do:

1. Season the ribs with salt, pepper, and brown sugar.
2. Place the rack of ribs in your slow cooker with the more meaty side facing the wall of the slow cooker. You will have to bend it and wrap it around the inside.
3. Pour BBQ sauce over the ribs.
4. Cook on low for 8 hours.

Slow Cooker Beef Burritos

Serves: 4-5

What you need:

- 2 lbs stew meat

- 1 large can enchilada sauce

- 1 beef bouillon

- 7 tortillas, burrito size

- 1 cup shredded cheddar cheese

What to do:

1. Place beef, enchilada sauce, and beef bouillon in the slow cooker and cook on low for 7-8 hours.
2. Shred the beef with a fork.
3. Spoon beef mixture onto each tortilla, add a couple tbsp of cheese to each, and roll up.
4. Place each burrito in a baking dish and broil for 3-4 minutes.

Slow Cooker Buffalo Ranch Wings

Servings: 2-4

What you need:

- 12-14 chicken wings

- 1 12-oz bottle of Frank's Red Hot Sauce

- 1 packet ranch dry seasoning

What to do:

1. Place the chicken wings in your slow cooker.
2. Cover and cook on high for 2-3 hours.
3. After 2-3 hours, drain the liquid out of the slow cooker.
4. In a small bowl, mix together the ranch seasoning and the hot sauce.
5. Pour this mixture over the chicken in the slow cooker.
6. Cover and cook for 1 hour.
7. Serve with your choice of dipping sauce.

Slow Cooker Chicken and Cheese

Servings: 4

What you need:

- 4 boneless, skinless chicken breasts

- 1 16-oz jar of salsa

- 4 slices provolone cheese

What to do:

1. Place the chicken breasts and salsa in your slow cooker. Cook for 4-5 hours or until the center of the chicken is no longer pink.
2. Spoon salsa over the top of the chicken and place a slice of cheese on each piece.

Slow Cooker Chicken Salsa Verde

Servings: 6

What you need:

- 6 chicken breasts

- 2 cups salsa verde

- 1 bottle of beer or 12 oz of chicken broth

- 2 tsp cumin

- 1 small can green chiles

What to do:

1. Place the chicken in your slow cooker and pour on the salsa verde and the beer or broth.
2. Sprinkle the chicken with cumin and pour the chiles on top.
3. Cook for 8 hours on low or 4 hours on high.
4. Shred the chicken with a fork.

Slow Cooker Cocktail Sausages

Servings: 6

What you need:

- 2 14-oz packages of cocktail smokies

- 18 oz jar of grape jelly

- 12 oz jar of chili sauce

- 1 tsp ground mustard

What to do:

1. Place all of the ingredients to your slow cooker.
2. Cook on low for 4 hours, stirring occasionally.

Slow Cooker Garlic Tilapia

Servings: 4

What you need:

- 4 tilapia filets

- 2 tbsp butter

- 1 tbsp minced garlic

- Salt and pepper, to taste

What to do:

1. Place the tilapia filets on a large sheet of aluminum foil.
2. Generously season each filet with salt and pepper.
3. Divide the butter and garlic between the four filets and top each of them.
4. Wrap the foil around the fish, sealing it as tightly as possible.
5. Place in your slow cooker and cook on high for 2 hours.

Slow Cooker Ham

Serves: 4-6

What you need:

- 1 precooked, spiral cut ham

- 2 cups brown sugar

- 1 can pineapple rings

What to do:

1. Sprinkle 1 and 1/2 cups of the brown sugar into the bottom of a slow cooker.
2. Place the ham on top of the brown sugar and pour the pineapple rings and juice on top.
3. Sprinkle the rest of the brown sugar on top of the ham.
4. Cook for 6-8 hours on low.

Slow Cooker Hawaiian BBQ Chicken

Servings: 6

What you need:

- 6 boneless, skinless chicken breasts

- 1 bottle Hawaiian style BBQ sauce

- 1 20 oz. can pineapple chunks

What to do:

1. Spray the inside of your slow cooker with cooking spray or insert a liner.
2. Place the chicken breasts in the slow cooker and cover with the BBQ sauce.
3. Pour the pineapple chunks on top of the chicken.
4. Cook on high for 2-3 hours or on low for 4-6 hours.
5. Shred the chicken with 2 forks then serve.

Slow Cooker Honey Garlic Chicken

Servings: 4

What you need:

- 4 boneless, skinless chicken breasts

- 1/2 cup A1 steak sauce

- 1/4 cup honey

- 1 tsp garlic powder

- 1/2 tsp hot sauce

What to do:

1. Place the chicken in your slow cooker.
2. Mix the steak sauce, honey, garlic powder, and hot sauce together in a small bowl.
3. Pour the mixture over the chicken.
4. Cook on low for 6 hours or until chicken is done and tender.

Slow Cooker Italian Chicken

Servings: 4

What you need:

- 4 boneless, skinless chicken breasts

- 1 can cheddar cheese soup

- 8 oz of zesty Italian dressing

What to do:

1. Add all 3 of the ingredients to your slow cooker.
2. Cook for 6 hours on low, stirring every couple of hours.

Slow Cooker Orange Chicken

Serves: 4

What you need:

- 3/4 cup orange marmalade

- 1 cup honey BBQ sauce

- 2 tbsp soy sauce

- 3 boneless, skinless chicken breasts

- Cooked rice

What to do:

1. Cut the chicken into bite sized pieces.
2. Place chicken pieces, marmalade, BBQ sauce, and soy sauce in a slow cooker and cook on low for 4 hours.
3. Serve over rice.

Slow Cooker Pork Chops

Servings: 6

What you need:

- 6 pork chops

- 1 package ranch dressing mix

- 2 cans cream of mushroom soup

What to do:

1. Place all of the ingredients into your slow cooker.
2. Cook on low for 7-8 hours, stirring occasionally.

Slow Cooker Pulled Pork

Serves: 2-4

What you need:

- 2-lb pork tenderloin

- 1 can root beer

- 1 18-oz bottle of bbq sauce

What to do:

1. Place the tenderloin in the slow cooker and pour the can of root beer over it.
2. Cook on low for 6 hours or until the pork shreds easily.
3. Drain off most of the root beer and shred pork completely with a fork.
4. Pour the bbq sauce over the pork and stir.
5. Cook on low for another hour or two before serving.

Slow Cooker Ranch Roast Beef

Servings: 6

What you need:

- 3lb boneless chuck roast

- 1 packet ranch seasoning

- 1 tsp garlic salt

- 6 French rolls

- 6 slices mozzarella cheese

What to do:

1. Place the chuck roast, ranch seasoning, and garlic salt in your slow cooker and cook for 8 hours on low.
2. Shred the beef with 2 forks and serve on French rolls topped with mozzarella cheese.

Slow Cooker Shredded BBQ Chicken

Servings: 4

What you need:

- 3 chicken breasts, cut in half

- 1 12-oz bottle of barbeque sauce

- 1/2 cup Italian dressing

- 1/4 cup brown sugar

- 2 tbsp Worcestershire sauce

What to do:

1. Place the chicken in your slow cooker.
2. In a medium bowl, whisk together the barbeque sauce, Italian dressing, brown sugar, and Worcestershire sauce.
3. Pour this mixture over the chicken.
4. Cook for 6-8 hours on low or 4 hours on high.
5. Shred the chicken with two forks.

Slow Cooker Spicy Meatballs

Servings: 6

What you need:

- 1 28-oz bag of fully cooked frozen meatballs

- 12 oz grape jelly

- 28 oz bbq sauce

- 2 habanero peppers

What to do:

1. Dice the habanero peppers very finely. Wear gloves!
2. Place all of the ingredients into your slow cooker.
3. Cook for 4 hours on low.

Slow Cooker Tangy Meatballs

Servings: 6

What you need:

- 28 oz of frozen fully cooked meatballs

- 18 oz jar of grape jelly

- 12 oz jar of chili sauce

- 1 tsp ground mustard

What to do:

1. Place all of the ingredients to your slow cooker.
2. Cook on low for 4 hours, stirring occasionally.

Slow Cooker Teriyaki Chicken

Servings: 2

What you need:

- 2 boneless, skinless chicken breasts

- 1 1/2 cups teriyaki Sauce

- 2 cups cooked rice

What to do:

1. Pound out the chicken until it is uniformly thin.
2. Lay the chicken breasts in the bottom of your slow cooker and cover with teriyaki sauce.
3. Cook on low for 6 hours or until chicken is tender and cooked.
4. Serve with rice.

Steak Dressing

Servings: 6

What you need:

- 2 lbs sirloin steak

- 1 box cornbread stuffing mix

- 1 can rotel tomatoes

- 1/2 stick of butter, melted

What to do:

1. Place the steak into your slow cooker.
2. In a medium bowl, stir together the stuffing, tomatoes, and butter
3. Pour the stuffing mixture over the steak in the slow cooker.
4. Cook on low for 8 hours or on high for 4 hours.

Sweet Heat Chicken

Servings: 4

What you need:

- 4 boneless, skinless chicken breasts

- 1 20-oz bottle sweet chili sauce

- 1 20-oz can crushed pineapples

- 1 red bell pepper, chopped

- 1 small onion, chopped

What to do:

1. Place all of the ingredients into your slow cooker.
2. Cook on low for 8 hours or on high for 4 hours, stirring occasionally.

DESSERTS

Bananas Foster

Serves: 4-6

What you need:

- 1 cup packed brown sugar

- 1/4 tsp cinnamon

- 1/2 cup butter, sliced

- 4 ripe bananas, peeled and sliced

- 1/4 cup dark rum

What to do:

1. Combine the brown sugar, cinnamon, and butter in your crock pot.
2. Cover and cook on low for an hour, stirring occasionally.
3. Add in the bananas and stir to coat evenly.
4. Stir in the rum.
5. Cover and cook for another 30 minutes.

Cake Balls

Makes 4 dozen

What you need:

- 1 16-oz box yellow cake mix, plus ingredients the directions call for

- Candy melts

- Sprinkles

- Skewers

What to do:

1. Preheat your oven to 350 degrees F.
2. Combine all of the cake mix ingredients according to the box directions.
3. Place the cake batter in pastry bag or a large zip lock bag with the tip cut off.
4. Pipe the batter into a cake pop pan that has been sprayed with non-stick spray.
5. Bake for 18-20 minutes.
6. Let the cake pop pan rest for 5 minutes before opening it.
7. Place the cake pops onto a wire cooling rack to cool completely.

8. While pops are cooling, melt the candy melts according to package directions.
9. Insert the tip of a skewer into the melted chocolate, then into a cake pop. This helps it stick better.
10. Dip each cake pop into the melted chocolate and coat well.
11. Sprinkle each covered cake pop with sprinkles then let dry on wax paper.

Chocolate Caramel Cake Cookies

Makes about 30 cookies

What you need:

- 1 box devil's food cake mix

- 2 eggs

- 1/2 cup canola oil

- 30 Rolo candies

- Christmas colored M&M's

What to do:

1. Preheat your oven to 350 degrees F and line two baking sheets with parchment paper.
2. In a large bowl, mix together the cake mix, eggs, and oil.
3. Roll the dough into tbsp sized balls and place 1 inch apart on the prepared baking sheets.
4. Press one Rolo into each ball.
5. Bake for 8-10 minutes.
6. As soon as you remove the cookies from the oven, press 4 M&M's onto each cookie then let cool.

Cake Batter Fudge

Servings: 8

What you need:

- 1 cup yellow cake mix

- 1 cup powdered sugar

- 1/2 stick of butter

- 1/4 cup milk

- 1/2 cup sprinkles

What to do:

1. Place all of the ingredients except the sprinkles in a microwave safe bowl and microwave for two minutes.
2. Remove from microwave and stir together well.
3. Stir in the sprinkles.
4. Pour into a greased square baking dish.
5. Cover and refrigerate for 2 hours.
6. Cut into squares once its refrigerated.

Brownies

Servings: 12

What you need:

- 9 oz semi-sweet chocolate chips

- 1 stick butter

- 1 cup sugar

- 2 eggs + 1 egg yolk

- 1 cup all-purpose flour

What to do:

1. Preheat your oven to 350 degrees F and spray an 8x8 dish with cooking spray.
2. In a microwave safe bowl, melt the chocolate chips and butter together in your microwave for 30 seconds or until completely melted. Just make sure you stir every 20-30 seconds.
3. Add in the sugar and mix well.
4. Add in the eggs, egg yolk, and flour. Stir with a wooden spoon until just combined.
5. Pour the batter into the prepared pan and bake for 25-30 minutes.
6. Cut and serve!

Coconut Balls

Servings: 8

What you need:

- 8 oz cream cheese, softened

- 1 tbsp butter, softened

- 4 cups powdered sugar

- 1 cup shredded coconut

- 1 tbsp shortening

- 2 cups chocolate chips

What to do:

1. Using an electric mixer, beat the cream cheese and butter together in a large bowl.
2. Add in the coconut and the powdered sugar, 1 cup at a time.
3. Cover and place the mixture in the refrigerator for 1 hour.
4. Line a large baking sheet with parchment paper.
5. Mold the mixture into balls and place them onto the baking sheet.
6. Place the baking sheet in the freezer for 2 hours.

7. Place the chocolate chips and shortening in a microwave safe bowl and heat 30 seconds at a time until completely melted. Stir occasionally.
8. Using a fork, dip the frozen coconut balls into the melted chocolate until they are completely coated. Return to the baking sheet to dry.

Chocolate Mousse

Servings: 4

What you need:

- 10 oz semi-sweet chocolate chips

- 1 cup water

- 4 tbsp sugar

What to do:

1. In a double boiler or a bowl placed over a pot of boiling water, melt the chocolate, water, and sugar together.
2. Fill a large bowl with ice. Place the bowl of melted chocolate/water/sugar in the bowl of ice (the whole bowl).
3. With an electric mixer, mix the chocolate mixture until it begins to thicken.
4. Serve immediately.

Chocolate Peanut Butter Bars

Servings: 12

What you need:

- 1 stick butter, softened

- 1 3/4 cups creamy peanut butter, divided

- 2 tsp vanilla

- 1 cup powdered sugar

- 3 cups chocolate chips, divided

What to do:

1. Line a square baking pan with parchment paper.
2. In a saucepan, melt together 2 tbsp of peanut butter and 1 1/2 cups of chocolate chips over low heat. When melted, pour this mixture into the prepared pan in an even layer. Cover and refrigerate for 30 minutes.
3. In a mixing bowl, with an electric mixer, whip together 1 1/2 cups of peanut butter, 1 stick of butter, vanilla extract, and powdered sugar until smooth and creamy.
4. Spoon this mixture over the chocolate layer in the prepared pan. Cover and refrigerate for another 30 minutes.

5. Melt the remaining peanut butter and 1 1/2 cups semi-sweet chocolate chips in a saucepan like you did in step 2. Pour this mixture over the peanut butter mixture in the pan. Cover and refrigerate for 1 hour before cutting and serving.

Blueberry Coconut Bars

Makes 15 squares

What you need:

- 2 cups sweetened coconut

- 2 cups blueberries

- 1/4 cup maple syrup

- 2 tsp ground vanilla beans

What to do:

1. Place all of the ingredients in your food processor and mix until smooth.
2. Line a square baking dish with parchment paper, extending it over the sides.
3. Pour the mixture into the baking dish and spread it evenly.
4. Gently press the mixture down using the extended sides of the parchment paper.
5. Refrigerate for 30 minutes, then slice and serve or store in the refrigerator in an airtight container.

Dr. Pepper Cherry Cobbler

Serves: 6-8

What you need:

- 1 21-oz can of cherry pie filling

- 1 boxed devil's food cake mix

- 1 20-oz bottle of Dr. Pepper

- 1/2 cup butter, sliced

What to do:

1. Pour the cherry pie filling into your crock pot and spread evenly.
2. Sprinkle the dry cake mix onto the cherries.
3. Evenly pour the Dr. Pepper over the cake mix.
4. Place the slices of butter over the mixture.
5. Cook on high for 2-3 hours.

Bird's Nests

Makes 30

What you need:

- 12 oz. package chow mein noodles

- 12 oz package of butterscotch chips

- 90 egg shaped candies (jelly beans, robin's eggs, etc.)

What to do:

1. Line a large baking sheet with parchment paper.
2. Melt the butterscotch chips in a microwave safe bowl in the microwave at 20 second increments until completely melted.
3. Pour the chow mein noodles into the melted butterscotch and stir to coat evenly.
4. Use a 1/4 cup measuring cup to portion out the mixture onto the baking sheet.
5. Place 3 egg candies on top of each "nest".
6. Allow the nests to set for 10-20 minutes.

Apple-Cherry Cobbler

Servings: 4-6

What you need:

- 1/2 cup granulated sugar

- 2 tbsp instant vanilla pudding mix

- 1 tsp apple pie spice

- 1 can apple pie mix

- 1 can cherries

What to do:

1. Place all of the ingredients into your crock pot and stir together well.
2. Cook on low for 4-5 hours.
3. Serve over ice cream.

Apple Spice Cake

Servings: 8-10

What you need:

- 2 16-oz cans of sliced apples

- 1 package spice cake mix

- 1 stick butter, melted

- 1/2 cup chopped pecans

What to do:

1. Spray your crock pot with non-stick cooking spray.
2. Pour the cans of apples into the crock pot and spread them evenly over the bottom.
3. Sprinkle the spice cake mix over the apples.
4. Pour the melted butter evenly over the dry mix.
5. Top with the chopped pecans.
6. Cook on low for 3-5 hours.
7. Serve with ice cream.

Apple Pecan Dump Cake

Servings: 4-6

What you need:

- 2 21-oz cans apple pie filling

- 1 box yellow cake mix

- 1 1/2 sticks of butter or margarine, melted

- 2 tsp cinnamon

- 1 cup chopped pecans

What to do:

1. Pour the apple pie filling into the bottom of your crock pot.
2. Sprinkle the cinnamon over the apples.
3. Evenly pour the cake mix over the apples.
4. Pour the melted butter over the cake mix evenly.
5. Sprinkle the pecans over the mixture.
6. Cook on high for 2 hours.
7. Serve with ice cream.

Fudge

Servings: 8-10

What you need:

- 1 cup dark chocolate chips

- 1 cup of coconut milk

- 1/4 cup of honey

What to do:

1. Mix the ingredients directly into your crock pot.
2. Cook on low for 2 hours.
3. Stir until the mixture is smooth.
4. Pour the fudge mixture into a greased casserole dish.
5. Cover the fudge with plastic wrap and refrigerate for at least 3 hours before serving.

Hot Fudge Sundae Cake

Serves: 6-8

What you need:

- 1 box chocolate cake mix, plus the ingredients the box instructions call for

- 1/2 cup chopped pecans

- 1 cup brown sugar

- 3 tbsp cocoa

- 1 3/4 cups hot water

What to do:

1. Mix the chocolate cake according to package directions.
2. Pour the batter into your crock pot.
3. Mix together the cocoa and brown sugar and pour the hot water over it and mix well.
4. Pour the cocoa/brown sugar mixture over the batter.
5. Sprinkle the chopped pecans into the crock pot.
6. Cook on high for 4 hours then serve.

Ice Cream Bread

Servings: 8

What you need:

- 1 pint of your favorite ice cream, softened

- 1 1/2 cups self-rising flour

What to do:

1. Preheat your oven to 350 degrees F and spray a 8x4 or 9x5 pan with cooking spray.
2. In a mixing bowl, with an electric mixer, mix together the softened ice cream and the flour until just combined.
3. Pour the mixture into the prepared pan and smooth out.
4. Bake for 40-45 minutes or until a toothpick inserted into the center comes out clean.
5. Remove from the oven and let it cool for 10 minutes before removing from the pan.

Oreo Cheesecake Cookies

Servings: 10-12

What you need:

- 4 oz cream cheese, softened

- 1 stick butter, softened

- 3/4 cup sugar

- 1 cup + 2 tbsp all-purpose flour

- 10 Oreos, crumbled

What to do:

1. Beat the cream cheese and butter together with a mixer until light and fluffy. Add in the sugar and beat well.
2. Add in the flour a little bit at a time and mix until just combined.
3. Stir in the Oreos.
4. Cover and refrigerate for 1 hour.
5. Before baking, preheat your oven to 350 degrees F.
6. Line a baking sheet with parchment paper.
7. Roll up two tablespoons of dough into a ball and place on the prepared sheet. Repeat until all dough is used
8. Bake for 10-11 minutes, edges will be golden and center still soft.

9. Cool for 10 minutes, then transfer to a wire rack to cool completely.

Oreo Lasagna

Servings: 10

What you need:

- 3 packages of Oreos

- 2 16-oz tubs of cool whip, thawed

- 12-oz cream cheese, softened

- 2 cups milk

- Chocolate sauce, for drizzling

What to do:

1. In the bowl of a stand mixer, whip the cream cheese until fluffy.
2. Spoon the cool whip into the cream cheese and mix well. Set aside.
3. Dip Oreos, one at a time, into the milk. Lay flat in the bottom of a 9x13 pan until an even layer covers the bottom.
4. Spread an even layer of cream cheese/cool whip mixture over the Oreos.
5. Repeat the layers 2 more times.
6. Drizzle with chocolate sauce.
7. Cover and refrigerate for 6 hours or overnight.

Oreo Truffles

Makes 12

What you need:

- 1 package Oreos

- 8-oz cream cheese

- 8-oz chocolate chips

- 4-oz white chocolate chips, melted

What to do:

1. Pulse the Oreos in your food processor until evenly crumbled. Add the cream cheese and pulse until smooth. Scrape down sides if necessary.
2. Portion the mixture with a 1/4 measuring cup and roll into egg shapes.
3. Place the eggs on a parchment paper lined baking sheet and refrigerate for 2 hours or freeze for 1 hour.
4. Melt the chocolate chips in a microwave safe bowl.
5. Dip the eggs into the melted chocolate and place back onto the baking sheet.
6. Place melted white chocolate chips into a piping bag or zip lock bag with a corner cut off.
7. Pipe designs onto the chocolate dipped eggs.
8. Let cool before serving.

Peach Dump Cake

Servings: 6-8

What you need:

- 1 box yellow cake mix

- 2 21-oz cans peach pie filling

- 1 stick butter, melted

What to do:

1. Empty the cans of peach pie filling into the bottom of your slow cooker and spread evenly.
2. In a mixing bowl, stir together the cake mix (just the mix) and the melted butter.
3. Crumple the cake/butter mixture over the peach filling and spread as evenly as possible.
4. Cook on high for 2 hours or on low for 4 hours.
5. Serve over ice cream, if desired.

Peanut Butter Cookie Mug Cake

Servings: 1

What you need:

- 1/4 cup creamy peanut butter

- 4 tbsp milk

- 4 tbsp all-purpose flour

- 1/2 tsp baking powder

What to do:

1. In a large microwave-safe mug, add the peanut butter, then milk, then flour, then baking powder.
2. Mix until no lumps remain.
3. Cook in the microwave for 1 minute and 20 seconds.
4. Let cool slightly then enjoy.

Peanut Butter Cookies

Servings: 12

What you need:

- 1 cup peanut butter

- 1 cup sugar

- 1 egg

- 1 tsp baking soda

What to do:

1. In a mixing bowl, combine the peanut butter, sugar, and egg well.
2. Mix in the baking soda.
3. Roll the dough into 1-inch balls.
4. Place the balls on a baking sheet sprayed with nonstick spray and bake for 8-10 minutes at 350 degrees F.

Pineapple Angel Food Trifle

Servings: 8-10

What you need:

- 1 oz box of instant vanilla pudding

- 20 oz can crushed pineapples

- 1 premade angel food cake

- 8 oz cool whip, thawed

- 12 oz frozen strawberry slices in syrup, thawed

What to do:

1. In a large bowl, mix together the vanilla pudding mix and the crushed pineapples (and juice).
2. Stir the cool whip into the pudding/pineapple mixture.
3. Crumble 1/3 of the angel food cake into the bottom of a bowl or trifle dish, then layer 1/3 of the pineapple/pudding mixture. Repeat the layers twice.
4. Top with strawberries and serve.

Pumpkin Pie Dip

Servings: 6-8

What you need:

- 2 cups canned pumpkin pie mix

- 8 oz cream cheese, cubed

- 1/2 cup sour cream

- Chopped pecans

What to do:

1. Add the pumpkin pie mix, cream cheese, and sour cream into your crock pot.
2. Cook for 1-2 hours on low then stir well. Make sure the cream cheese is melted completely. If its not, cook until it is.
3. Top with chopped pecans.
4. Serve with apple slices, pretzels, cookies, or whatever you want.

Red Velvet Cookies

Makes 2 dozen

What you need:

- 1 box red velvet cake mix

- 6 tbsp butter, melted

- 1 cup powdered sugar

- 1 tsp cornstarch

- 2 eggs

What to do:

1. Preheat your oven to 375 degrees F and line a baking sheet with parchment paper.
2. Combine the cornstarch and powdered sugar in a small bowl.
3. In a large bowl, combine the cake mix, melted butter, and eggs. Mix on low with an electric mixer.
4. Roll into 1-inch balls and roll in the powdered sugar/cornstarch mixture.
5. Place balls 2-inches apart on the prepared baking sheet.
6. Bake for 9-11 minutes or until set.
7. Let cool on the baking sheets for 5 minutes before transferring to a wire rack to cool completely.

S'mores Cups

Servings: 12

What you need:

- 7 whole graham crackers, finely crushed

- 1/4 cup powdered sugar

- 1 stick of butter, melted

- 2 Hershey's chocolate bars

- 12 large marshmallows

What to do:

1. Preheat your oven to 350 degrees F and spray a mini muffin pan with nonstick spray.
2. Combine the graham cracker crumbs, powdered sugar, and melted butter in a bowl.
3. Scoop 1 tablespoonful of the crumb mixture into each cup of the prepared mini muffin pan.
4. Press the crumbs into the cups to make a cup.
5. Bake for 5 minutes.
6. Break the chocolate bars into 24 individual rectangles.
7. Place one rectangle in each graham cracker crust cup.
8. Cut each marshmallow in half and place half a marshmallow on top of each piece of chocolate.

9. Bake for 3 minutes.
10. Turn broiler on for 1 minute or until the marshmallows appear roasted.

S'mores Dessert

Servings: 8-10

What you need:

- 1 chocolate cake box mix

- Ingredients the box mix calls for

- 2 cups mini marshmallows

- 1 1/2 cups milk chocolate chips

- 6 graham crackers

What to do:

1. Mix the cake mix according to box directions.
2. Spray the bottom of your crock pot with non-stick spray.
3. Add half the of the cake batter to the crock pot.
4. Add 1 cup of marshmallows and 1 cup of chocolate chips to the crock pot.
5. Add a layer of graham crackers.
6. Pour on the rest of the batter.
7. Cook on low for 2 hours.
8. Add the rest of the marshmallows and chocolate and finish off with crumbled crackers on top.
9. Cook for another 30 minutes before serving.

Slow Cooker Apple Dump Cake

Servings: 4-6

What you need:

- 21 oz can of apple pie filling

- 1 15-oz yellow cake mix

- 1 stick butter

- 1/2 cup walnuts

What to do:

1. Pour the apple pie filling into your slow cooker.
2. Sprinkle the cake mix over the apples.
3. Cut the butter into slices and put over the cake mix.
4. Sprinkle on the walnuts.
5. Cook on low for 4 hours.

Slow Cooker Blueberry Cobbler

Servings: 4-6

What you need:

- 1 18-oz yellow cake mix

- 3 cups frozen or fresh blueberries

- 1 stick butter

- 1/4 tsp cinnamon

What to do:

1. Place the blueberries in your slow cooker.
2. Sprinkle the cake mix onto the blueberries.
3. Slice the butter and put it over the cake mix.
4. Sprinkle with cinnamon.
5. Cook on low for 4 hours.

Slow Cooker Bread Pudding

Serves: 4-6

What you need:

- 10 slices raisin cinnamon swirl bread, cut into cubes
- 1 14-oz can sweetened condensed milk
- 1 cup water
- 1 tsp vanilla
- 5 eggs, beaten

What to do:

1. Place the bread cubes into your slow cooker.
2. Mix the sweetened condensed milk, water, vanilla, and eggs together in a bowl and pour the mixture over the bread.
3. Stir to coat the bread evenly.
4. Cook on low for 3-4 hours or until set.

Slow Cooker Cherry Dump Cake

Servings: 4-6

What you need:

- 21 oz can of cherry pie filling

- 1 15-oz yellow cake mix

- 1 stick butter

- 1/2 cup walnuts

What to do:

1. Pour the cherry pie filling into your slow cooker.
2. Sprinkle the cake mix over the cherries.
3. Cut the butter into slices and put over the cake mix.
4. Sprinkle on the walnuts.
5. Cook on low for 4 hours.

Slow Cooker Peach Cobbler

Servings: 4-6

What you need:

- 1 18-oz yellow cake mix

- 3 cups frozen or fresh peaches, sliced

- 1 stick butter

- 1/4 tsp cinnamon

What to do:

1. Place the peaches in your slow cooker.
2. Sprinkle the cake mix onto the peaches.
3. Slice the butter and put it over the cake mix.
4. Sprinkle with cinnamon.
5. Cook on low for 4 hours.

Strawberry Whip

Servings: 4

What you need:

- 2 cups frozen sliced strawberries

- 1/4 cup canned coconut milk

- 1 1/2 tsp sugar

- 2 tsp lemon juice

What to do:

1. Place all of the ingredients into your blender and blend until smooth.
2. Serve immediately.

White Chocolate Oreo Fudge

Makes 32 squares

What you need:

- 1 can sweetened condensed milk
- 3 cups white chocolate chips
- 15 Oreos, roughly chopped

What to do:

1. Line an 8x8 dish with parchment paper. Cut the paper long enough to hang over the edges.
2. In a microwave safe bowl, microwave the white chocolate chips and sweetened condensed milk for 3 minutes, stirring every 30 seconds. Continue for longer if it's no completely melted.
3. Stir half of the chopped Oreos in to the melted chocolate.
4. Spread the mixture evenly into the prepared dish and top with the remaining Oreos.
5. Cover and refrigerate for at least 4 hours.
6. Pull the fudge out of the dish by the overhanging parchment paper and cut into squares.

FREE GIFT

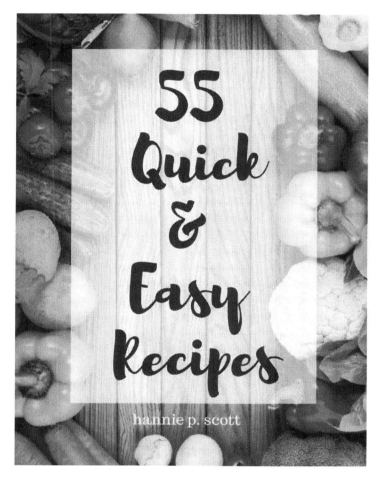

Breakfast, Lunch, Dinner, Soups, Salads, Desserts and More!

To download your free eBook, simply visit:
www.Hanniepscott.com/freegift

NOTES

NOTES

NOTES

NOTES

Made in the USA
Middletown, DE
28 February 2018